Life Is
God's
Best Gift

Life Is God's Best Gift

WISDOM FROM THE ANCESTORS

ON FINDING PEACE AND JOY

IN TODAY'S WORLD

Sam Chege, PhD

Amistad

An Imprint of HarperCollins*Publishers*

HarperCollins books may be purchased for educational, business, or sales promotional use. For information, please email the Special Markets Department at SPsales@harpercollins.com.

FIRST EDITION

Illustration on page ii: Tasha Drik / Shutterstock
All other illustrations: Shutterstock

Library of Congress Cataloging-in-Publication Data

Names: Chege, Sam, compiler.
Title: Life is God's best gift : wisdom from the ancestors on finding peace and joy in today's world / Sam Chege, Ph.D.
Other titles: Wisdom from the ancestors on finding peace and joy in today's world
Description: First edition. | New York, NY : HarperCollins Publishers, 2019.
Identifiers: LCCN 2018060270 (print) | LCCN 2019000899 (ebook) | ISBN 9780062906892 (eb) | ISBN 9780062906878 (hc : alk. paper)
Subjects: LCSH: Proverbs, African.
Classification: LCC PN6519.A6 (ebook) | LCC PN6519.A6 C44 2019 (print) | DDC 398.9096—dc23
LC record available at https://lccn.loc.gov/2018060270

---

19 20 21 22 23   LSC   10 9 8 7 6 5 4 3 2 1

To my late grandparents
Hannah Wachuka Chege and Samson Chege Kamau,
who raised me and shared with me deep cultural
wisdom that I may in turn share with others.
Fare thee well.
The fire you lit burns on!

A book is like a garden in the pocket.

Contents

Introduction

Scandal of Simplicity

I have lived a wonderful life. I was born and raised in Kenya, in an African village. My home was made of mud and had no electricity, running water, or indoor toilet. Next to my bedroom was a hearth and an indoor goat shed. The animals gave us milk, and on big occasions that called for a feast, they would give us their meat. This description of my surroundings may evoke images of deprivation and neglect. But, I assure you, it was the best life. And, it was the best life because it was a simple life. Most people would equate materialism with happiness and find it scandalous that one would find contentment in a simple life.

However, my family did not know we were poor. Our world was a place of communion, where everyone poured out their love and humanity and neighborliness into a pot from which we all drank to our fill. We were a community that shared everything we had with one another. Nobody went to bed hungry. The houses stood close to each other, separated by about ten feet. If you did not have salt or sugar, you sent your child to your neighbor's house, and your child never came back empty-handed.

At night the sound of children playing outside under the African moonlight captured the vibrant and carefree spirit of our youth. The moon was all we needed—and each other. It would take another thirty years before electricity found its way to the village and lit the night. But, in those days, we never missed it.

In the morning, we all walked to school barefoot, a sea of ironed school uniforms marching toward our destiny. Parents who wanted their kids to study hard and make a better life for themselves always pointed to the principal as the role model. His life and position in society were a testament to the value of education and its potential to change lives.

In my village there were a few hundred people. The principal happened to be one of the most educated people in the village. He along with other teachers who taught us in elementary school had the best houses, with indoor plumbing, bathrooms, and personal generators for electricity while the rest of us lived in mud houses. In my village, there was one car and it belonged to the school principal. The rest of us either walked wherever we went or took public transport if we needed to cover long distances.

When emergencies struck, people would knock on the principal's door for help. He never turned anyone away. Pregnant women whose time to deliver had come, or parents of sick kids who would never have made it through the night—he took them all in and delivered them to the hands of doctors many miles away in the deep of the night. He never charged anyone for his services.

It was a simple life—a scandalously simple life.

But it was the time I spent with my grandparents that made this simple life meaningful for me. In most African societies, the elderly are revered and sit at the pinnacle of the family structure. It has been assumed that wisdom comes with age. There is a famous African proverb that says, "An elder who is sitting down on a stool can see farther than a young boy perched in a tree." In other words, those who have lived long have more experiences in life. Youth are encouraged to consult them to learn about life. Wisdom is a treasure that our ancestors have handed down to us in the form of wise sayings, judicious encouragements, lived experiences, and proverbs.

Those who listen to the elders pave their own road to success. Reverence for the elderly not only enables you to receive wisdom from them but also honors the natural order of the society as expressed in another philosophical but popular African proverb: "Where is the house where the mouse is the leader?" In other words, the young (the mouse) do not reign while the elders are still alive.

Among my people, it is customary for a child to live with aging grandparents and to run their errands, perform minor chores, and do other tasks to help them age gracefully. It was a position of privilege and honor that opened a whole new world to me.

In Africa we have a saying that one who is raised by grandparents knows deep culture. Grandparents are the repositories of culture and history. Storytelling is a form of oral tradition that allows one generation to pass on knowledge and wisdom to the next generation, and I spent my evenings around the fire listening to them tell me stories. I was mesmerized by the profound history, rich insight, and depth of knowledge my elders had to share.

I was especially intrigued by the proverbs. They were succinct and loaded. They reminded me of an onion. Each proverb was packed with layers of profound understanding. I could just keep peeling away at each one and come to a higher and higher level of comprehension. Collectively, the proverbs helped me appreciate where I came from, create a professionally rewarding life, bond with my community, and give back to society. My fascination with the proverbs took me on a journey of discovery, gathering proverbs from all over Africa, as I wanted to help others to live a satisfying life.

I have collected thousands of proverbs over the years and I am constantly in awe of their power to focus my attention on what is important in life. *Life Is God's Best Gift* is the result of my work and my gift to you—ancient wisdom meant to be shared. In traditional African societies, fire was produced from a special wood or stone and community members could take it from anyone who had it. I'm passing along this flame of wisdom to you.

I have selected a representative sample of proverbs from various countries throughout Africa. Given the history of early migrations, similar proverbs exist throughout the continent in a variety of versions, each country using images drawn from the local environment. The continent of Africa is where knowledge, art, music, trade, and agriculture first flourished, and where even today natural resources abound. *Life Is God's Best Gift* is a treasure and an example of Africa's wealth. A rich harvest that will fill your soul and influence every aspect of your life, this delightful compendium of more than 300 pearls of wisdom will inspire purpose every day. Read one proverb each day for one year and apply the insight to your life, and I guarantee that after 365 days your spirit will be renewed. Trust me, the ancestors will shine light on your path.

This collection is arranged into six parts. "Aligning with Your Life's Purpose" is the first section. In African worldview, the individual is intimately connected to the community but has individual agency and efficacy that can promote the welfare of the community. And since the community is the sum total of its members, the conduct and character of individuals is the foundation of the community. Another part, "Awareness of the World Around You," teaches you how to align yourself with positive values so you can take your rightful place as a valued member of your community and, indeed, of the human race.

Through these proverbs, I share life's most important values, offering principles on ways to establish a life of substance and fulfillment. For example, the village life taught me that regardless of our station in life, our stories start and end the same way—with birth and death. It is what you do in between that sets you apart. In the section titled "Embracing Yourself," I encourage you to let your actions be the garlands that etch your name in eternal memory. In a world that judges the value of people based on their material possessions and other trappings of modernity, the village places a premium on character. For as the proverb says, "Wealth and fine clothes do not make character." From your ancestors comes your name, but your honor comes from your virtue. In this invaluable guide, these ancient proverbs ask you to make every day of your life a page of your history.

The late Professor Wangari Muta Maathai says it another way: "Be the difference maker and do the best you can." In 2004, she became the first African woman to receive the Nobel Peace Prize for her contribution to sustainable development, democracy, and peace. Among her best-known stories describing her view of life was one about the hummingbird. It is the story of a huge forest that was being consumed by a raging fire. All the animals of the forest looked on in fear feeling helpless and overwhelmed by the sheer size and ferociousness of the fire. But a little hummingbird decided to act. She flew to the nearest stream and came back with some water, which she poured on the fire. She went back and forth, back and forth, back and forth multiple times trying to fight the fire. All the other animals stood by watching. Doing nothing. They tried to discourage the hummingbird from fetching water, arguing that she was too small to make a difference. But the hummingbird responded: I am doing the best I can.

We should be like the hummingbird and always do the best we can and show patience with others in knowing that they are doing the same. We may be small and insignificant but we should not stand around doing nothing, expecting well-being and contentment to fall into our laps.

The village life also taught us that you can never truly be happy when your neighbor is hurting. When we place a premium on individual happiness, we don't even have to know our neighbor's name. And it is okay to bowl alone! A culture of individualism sometimes makes it hard to communicate with each other, even in a crisis situation. Africans believe in the necessity of discourse. We know that spending time chatting about big and small events alleviates loneliness and depression. Connections can be made in serving a cup of tea, coffee, or palm wine or a warm embrace. All of these methods demonstrate an inexpensive way to spread joy. Communing with society promotes harmony in one's life and throughout the community. Why would we need icebreakers when there is no ice between us?

"Gifting Yourself to Others" addresses our intimate and romantic relationships. As we all know, love is the most precious form of engagement with those around us. Who we love and how we demonstrate our love determines our level of happiness. I'm sure you have heard the saying, "A happy wife is a happy life." When we feel good in our relationships, it makes every aspect of our lives better. Our intimate relationships are the anchors that prime us to interact with the rest of the community.

In "Your Sense of Passion" you will discover advice on navigating your career and work life. It offers insight into entrepreneurship as well as into the focus and commitment needed to achieve this goal. The proverbs touch upon ignoring the distractions and allowing stumbling blocks to be used as stepping-stones to reach your prize. They offer suggestions, such as it is the little things that make big things happen—meaning that a mountain is composed of little grains of the earth, that you cannot have the ocean without the rivers. Chase your dreams with stubborn optimism and view every obstacle as an opportunity.

Our ancestors had a natural curiosity and a passion for information. The final section, "A Love of Knowing," shares the splendor of living a life seeking knowledge. It's necessary that you value intellect and wisdom, as culture and identity are essential tools in shaping who we are in our understanding of the world around us. This section includes insights about never leaving behind the love from which you came; not living for immediate gratification; becoming someone with the qualities you want to embrace; and not letting others define you. It is necessary that you cherish your heritage and do not become like water, which takes the tint of all colors.

Nowadays, I can afford almost anything I want and I am happy and grateful. But the modest life in the village remains the best life I ever lived. I still find the most joy, contentment, and happiness from engaging in conversations with friends, volunteering at a food bank, reading and enriching my mind, and doing other endeavors that involve giving of myself. Today, we tend to define ourselves by what we have and what we do, not who we are. We judge people by how they dress, what they drive, and where they live. The scandal of simplicity is in not allowing yourself to be defined by these things but by your relationship to yourself, nature, and fellow members of your community. Simplicity strips life of all its trappings and focuses our attention on the essence of life. Know that "Life is God's best gift; the rest is what you make of it."

1

Aligning with Your Life's Purpose

A man from the village went to the chief and asked permission to marry his beautiful daughter. The chief had a single requirement.

"Position yourself near the fence," he said. "I'm going to release three different bulls, one at a time. If you can catch the tail of one of the bulls, then you can marry my daughter."

The man stood by the fence as he was told. Out of the gate came the chief's strongest bull. Breathing fire, the bull aimed straight for the man. The man quickly climbed the fence to get out of the way, thinking the next bull had to be a little weaker.

The second bull came full speed, huffing and puffing. Again, the man moved out of the way. He convinced himself that the third bull had to be easier to handle.

The man saw the third bull enter the gate. Sure enough, the third bull was small, weak, and could barely run. The man thanked his lucky stars, as he waited for the bull's approach. As the bull passed by, the man grabbed at his backside. There was no tail!

In life we come across many opportunities.
The way in which we respond to
them determines our destiny.

A man who says it cannot
be done should not interrupt
the man doing it.

SWAZILAND

The poorest person is not
the one without money but
one without vision.

GHANA

We will water the thorn
for the sake of the rose.

CHAD AND LIBYA

*Ignore the distractions and
focus on the goal.*

By trying often, the monkey
learns to jump from tree
to tree without falling.

NIGERIA

Old men sit in the shade
because they planted a tree
many years before.

UGANDA

The sun does not forget a village
just because it is small.

MALI

*Success in life is not
determined by your size.*

God speaks to those who are
silent enough to listen.

ZAMBIA

A fly that has no one
to advise it follows the
corpse into the grave.

GAMBIA

He who looks for honey
must have the courage
to face the bees.

SEYCHELLES

*There is a cost for anything
valuable in life.*

You must attend to your business with the vendor in the market, and not to the noise of the market.

BENIN

Focus.

A pygmy's shadow is greater
with the setting sun.

DEMOCRATIC REPUBLIC
OF THE CONGO

*A worker's merits are often only
recognized after they leave.*

Work is good as long as
you don't forget to live.

RWANDA

*There is more to life than
making money.*

The eyes of a frog cannot
prevent a cow from drinking
water in the river.

KENYA

*We shall not be distracted
by naysayers.*

If you are not able to build a house
now, you could build a shed.

MOZAMBIQUE

Advice is a stranger—
if he's welcome he stays for
the night; if not, he
leaves the same day.

MADAGASCAR

A man does not go far from
where his corn is roasting.

NIGERIA

*Do not abandon that place where your sustenance
comes from. A man who patiently roasts his corn
by the side of the road knows that at the end of the
day, his loyalty to his occupation will be rewarded
and he will earn a living from selling his corn
to passersby. Remain loyal to your livelihood.*

Send a boy where he wants to
go and you'll see his best pace.

NIGERIA

You always learn a lot
more when you lose
than when you win.

LIBERIA

A good wind is no good to a sailor
who doesn't know his direction.

EQUATORIAL GUINEA

A cow that is in a hurry
to go to America will
return as corned beef.

NIGERIA

With gold you can make a road
to heaven but it will end in hell.

TOGO

*Great wealth brings with it
many distractions.*

If you want to give God
a good laugh, tell him of
your future plans.

NAMIBIA

It is not enough to run;
one must arrive and know
when one has arrived.

NIGERIA

Food that is meant for a tortoise
will never be hung on a tree.

SEYCHELLES AND ZAMBIA

There are many colorful flowers
on the path of life, but the prettiest
have the sharpest thorns.

MADAGASCAR

I pointed out to you the
stars and all you saw was
the tip of my finger.

TANZANIA

Do not be a miser who
saves his money for those
who will bury him.

MADAGASCAR

If you don't know where
you are going, any road
will take you there.

UGANDA

Money can't talk, yet it can
make lies look good.

SOUTH AFRICA

Never mind if your nose
is ugly, as long as you can
breathe through it.

ZAIRE

When a road is good, it is
used a second time.

ERITREA

No man can paddle
two canoes at the same time.

NIGERIA

You have to look after wealth,
but knowledge looks after you.

ZAMBIA

Those who accomplish
great things pay attention
to little ones.

MALI

The key that unlocks is
also the key that locks.

ALGERIA

*What you see as an obstacle
is also a solution.*

One does not forgo sleeping
because of the possibility
of nightmares.

UGANDA

By coming and going,
a bird constructs its nest.

GHANA

It is for saying that he has no time
that the monkey's body became
overgrown with long hairs.

NIGERIA

Do not overlook important tasks.

Strategy is better
than strength.

NIGERIA

Make money but don't
let money make you.

TANZANIA

If you are a leader, be like the
moon, not like the sun.

DEMOCRATIC REPUBLIC
OF THE CONGO

*Effective leaders do not
hog the limelight.*

One does not follow the
footprints in the water.

UGANDA

If you are trying to help me,
do so in a way that I can see.

If you are a flag, follow the wind.

TANZANIA AND KENYA

*A person who has no convictions
will waver depending on the
time and circumstances.*

The forest provides food
to the hunter after he is
utterly exhausted.

ZIMBABWE

Blood is the sweat of heroes.

ZIMBABWE

If you wish to move mountains
tomorrow, you must start
by lifting stones today.

EQUATORIAL GUINEA

By pounding the dough,
the bread will rise.

SOUTH AFRICA

A man is as big as his ambitions.

GUINEA

You can only see what your
mind can comprehend.

Almost is not eaten.

SOUTH AFRICA

He who keeps trying
gets the reward.

ZAMBIA

The big fish is caught
with big bait.

SIERRA LEONE

Seize opportunity by the chin
for it is bald behind.

KENYA

If you are going to bathe,
get thoroughly wet.

MALAWI

If you decide to do something,
go all the way.

The path is made by walking.

God is good, but never
dance with a lion.

Do not set sail using
someone else's star.

NIGERIA

If things are getting easier,
maybe you are headed
downhill.

GHANA

The rich man never dances badly.

RWANDA

Wealth conceals flaws.

A large chair does not
make a king.

SUDAN

*There is more to leadership than
the trappings of the office.*

One who runs alone
cannot be outrun.

ETHIOPIA

Don't despise the nut;
one day it will be a palm tree.

ANGOLA

If you are on a road to
nowhere, find another road.

UGANDA

Many words do not fill a basket.

BENIN

Empty words are not eaten.
We have to work to eat.

Water always finds a way out.

CAMEROON

*There is a solution for
every problem.*

2

Embracing
Yourself

A boy in the village constantly complained that he had only one pair of shoes. So his dad took him on a city tour for a day. In the streets of the city, the boy was shocked to see a beggar who had no legs. His dad asked, "Son, what do you think that man would wish for: legs or shoes?"

"Legs," said the boy.

"You see, you are a lucky boy," said the father. "You have both your legs and a pair of shoes on."

The boy never complained again.

*Learn to enjoy what you have even
as you aim for what you don't.*

If you think you are too small to make a difference, you haven't spent a night with a mosquito.

BOTSWANA AND SWAZILAND

When the head is too big,
it cannot dodge blows.

MAURITIUS AND ZAMBIA

People who drink to drown
their sorrows should be told that
sorrow knows how to swim.

SIERRA LEONE

A lie can destroy a
thousand truths.

GHANA

When the moon is not full, the
stars shine more brightly.

UGANDA

He that forgives
gains victory.

SOUTH AFRICA

The wind does not break
a tree that bends.

TANZANIA

He who is courteous
is not a fool.

NIGERIA

The same boiling water
that softens potatoes
also hardens eggs.

MALI

We are forged not by the situation
but by our character. Circumstances
test our character and bring forth
what we are made of.

If you don't stand for something,
you will fall for anything.

MALAWI

The death that will kill a
man begins as an appetite.

NIGERIA

Words are like eggs:
when they are hatched,
they have wings.

MADAGASCAR

A monkey does not see his
own behind (backside);
he sees his neighbor's.

ZIMBABWE

When a man is stung,
he does not destroy
all the beehives.

KENYA

*Your reaction should be
proportionate to events.*

No matter how hot your anger is,
it cannot cook yams.

NIGERIA

*Too much anger can limit your
ability to move on with life.*

It is what is in the heart when
there is no wine in the hand
that comes out when there
is wine in the head.

NIGERIA

*Wine opens the gates to
tightly held secrets.*

A man's wealth may be
superior to him.

GABON

A bad name is like a stigma.

BENIN

If a man wants to grow a
long tooth, he should have
the lip to cover it.

CHAD

*Be sure you can shoulder the
blessing you are praying for.*

You can measure the
depth of the sea but not the
depth of a man's heart.

MALAWI

When the roots of a tree
begin to decay, it spreads
death to the branches.

NIGERIA

A man with too much ambition

cannot sleep in peace.

GUINEA-BISSAU

Moderation balances our desires.

A roaring lion kills no game.

Silence is a strategy.
Action speaks louder
than words.

An elephant which kills
a rat is not a hero.

CAMEROON

Your actions must be just.

When all men say you are
a dog, it is time to bark.

TOGO

Accept genuine criticism.

When a monkey climbs a
tree, its bottom becomes more
exposed the higher it goes.

MALAWI

If you do not have patience,
you cannot make beer.

NAMIBIA

If you fear something,
you give it power over you.

CHAD

He who tells the truth
is never wrong.

TANZANIA

A stubborn person sails
in a clay boat.

TANZANIA

*Sometimes people who don't
listen to advice have to
learn the hard way.*

A monkey leaps only as
far as it can reach.

SEYCHELLES

One's manner is like seeds
on a windy day; they
spread far and wide.

NIGERIA

Do not say the first thing
that comes to your mind.

KENYA

A man who uses force is
afraid of reasoning.

KENYA

When you shoot a zebra
in the black stripe, the
white stripe dies, too.

SOUTH AFRICA

We are the sum of our selves.

When a ripe fruit sees an
honest man, it drops.

LESOTHO

Honesty has its rewards.

A parasite cannot live alone.

NAMIBIA

When deed speaks,
words are nothing.

KENYA

If the owner of a calabash deems
it worthless, others will join him
and use it to pack rubbish.

GAMBIA

A too modest man goes hungry.

ETHIOPIA

You cannot expect to be cured if
you conceal your illness.

One head does not contain
all the wisdom.

No man is an island.

Do not respond to a mosquito
with a hammer because you will
miss and hurt yourself.

KENYA

*Each problem requires
an equal solution.*

No matter the color of the cow,
the milk is always white.

GAMBIA

By crawling, a child
learns to stand.

GHANA

It is one's deeds that are
counted, not one's years.

GHANA AND IVORY COAST

It is crooked wood that
shows the best sculptor.

BURKINA FASO

An elephant never fails
to carry its tusk.

KENYA AND TANZANIA

We are equal to our tasks.

Not all the flowers of a
tree produce fruit.

MAURITANIA

*The womb that produces a king
also produces a beggar.*

The sheep that wants to grow a
long horn must have a strong skull.

MAURITANIA

*Before you pray, be sure you can
bear what you are asking for.*

Giant silk cotton trees grow
out of very tiny seeds.

GAMBIA

We should put out fire
while it is still small.

KENYA

Free things decrease
one's intelligence.

BURUNDI

Dependence is disabling.

Even the Niger River must
flow around an island.

Be humble.

A tree that has twisted
for thirty years cannot be
straightened in a single day.

GHANA

It is hard to change as an adult.

Do not blame God for having
created the tiger, but thank Him
for not having given it wings.

ETHIOPIA

That which you condone,
you cannot change.

KENYA

Ugly caterpillars become
beautiful butterflies with
the turn of the seasons.

TANZANIA

Wherever man goes to dwell,
his character goes with him.

EQUATORIAL GUINEA

If you are bathing in the river
and a crazy fellow comes
along and steals your clothes,
and you run after him
naked, you too run the risk
of being taken as insane.

KENYA

3

Awareness of the World Around You

A driver in Zimbabwe was asked to drive an international visitor to a town deep in the rural areas. It so happened that the town was near the driver's village. So, he decided to stop by and say hello to his family. The driver and visitor were met by a strange sight. A huge crowd had gathered in the driver's village and everyone was haggling excitedly. It looked like they had wandered into a political rally or a religious gathering.

It turns out the village had been terrorized by a rogue elephant. They had just received word from the village chief that a ranger was on the way to shoot it. Soon there would be a lot of meat for everyone. The excited villagers had gathered at the chief's office to decide how the meat would be divided to ensure that each household would get a fair share.

The humanity of the village justice system was on full display.

The man who remembers others
remembers also his creator.

Until the lions have their own
historians, tales of hunting will
always glorify the hunter.

NIGERIA

We do not inherit the earth
from our ancestors; we borrow
it from our children.

ZIMBABWE

The one-eyed man does not thank
God until he sees a blind man.

GHANA

Beyond your sphere, your
importance wanes.

ANGOLA

No matter how long a log
stays in the water, it will
never become a crocodile.

MALI

If you cut your chains, you
free yourself. If you cut
your roots, you die.

GHANA

A teacher will appear when
the student is ready.

MOROCCO

Return to watering holes
for more than water; friends and
dreams are there to meet you.

BOTSWANA

He who thinks he is leading
and has no one following
him is only taking a walk.

MALAWI

*You are a leader through
other people.*

The real journey of discovery
begins in old age.

ANGOLA

When you climb the mountain
and reach the top, do not
forget the branches and shrubs
that helped your footing.

SOUTH AFRICA

When you straighten up your
back, no man can ride you.

CENTRAL AFRICAN REPUBLIC

No matter how tall a man
may be, he can never
see tomorrow.

NIGERIA

A man who prides himself
on his ancestry only is like
a potato plant, the best part
of which is underground.

SWAZILAND

A child cannot pay for
her mother's milk.

NIGERIA

When one is born, he is
already old enough to die.

You can outrun what is running
after you, but not what is
running inside of you.

A diamond's father is coal
yet it regards itself as upper class.

NAMIBIA

Never forget your humble beginnings,
no matter how high you rise.

The ruin of a nation begins
in the homes of its people.

GHANA

*The family is the foundation
of society.*

A silly daughter teaches her
mother how to bear children.

ETHIOPIA

Do not forget what it is
like to be a sailor because
you are now a captain.

TANZANIA

The multitude is stronger
than the king.

TUNISIA

You know what to say,
but you do not know what
you might be told.

TANZANIA AND KENYA

Gone are the days when boys
used to take off their hats when
greeting elders; these days they
just remove one earphone.

NIGERIA

It is not what you call me,
but what I answer to.

NIGERIA

People say that slaves were
taken from Africa. This is not
true. People were taken from
Africa and made into slaves.

BENIN

Before starting to sing,
the young bird will listen
to the song of the old.

NIGER

A man without culture is like
a zebra without stripes.

KENYA AND TANZANIA

When an old man dies,
a library burns to the ground.

GAMBIA

We desire to bequest two
things to our children—
the first one is roots;
the other one is wings.

SUDAN

However far the stream flows,
it never forgets its source.

NIGERIA

It takes a village to raise a child.

NIGERIA

It is easy to become a
monk in one's old age.

GABON

The future emerges from the past.

SENEGAL

If you know his father and
grandfather, you may trust his son.

MOROCCO

The old woman looks after
the child to grow its teeth
and the young one looks
after the old woman when
she loses her teeth.

GHANA

A mother is like a kernel,
crushed by problems but strong
enough to overcome them.

DEMOCRATIC REPUBLIC
OF THE CONGO

If two wise men always agree,
then there is no need
for one of them.

ZAMBIA

Knowledge comes from diversity of thought.

You have little power over
what's not yours.

ZIMBABWE

Respect boundaries.

The wise aim at boundaries
beyond the present; they transcend
the parameters of their origins.

CAMEROON

Youths talk first and then listen;
the elderly listen and then talk.

LESOTHO

No matter how many times
you wash a goat, it will
still smell like a goat.

ETHIOPIA

You are who you are.

Even in old age, the lion lives
with power and strength.

CENTRAL AFRICAN REPUBLIC

Knowledge is like a garden:
if it is not cultivated, it
cannot be harvested.

GUINEA

No matter how many house
chores you complete, there
are always more to be done.

MALI

Matters of the home are unending.

To kiss the child
is to kiss the mother.

BOTSWANA

The road to a mother's heart
passes through her child.

A zebra takes its stripes
wherever it goes.

TANZANIA AND KENYA

An elder who is sitting down
on a stool can see farther than a
young boy perched in a tree.

NIGERIA

If you are in hiding,
don't light a fire.

GHANA

A tree is strong because
of its roots.

ZAMBIA

Train a child the way he
should go and make sure
you also go the same way.

NIGERIA

Model your lessons.

A monkey that lives amongst
dogs learns how to bark.

NIGERIA

A man who has not prepared
his children for his eventual
death has failed as a father.

LESOTHO

What the child says,
he has heard at home.

NIGERIA

Kids learn from their parents.
Model what you want your
kids to become.

It takes a vulture to shave
another vulture.

MOZAMBIQUE

When you change kings,
you change customs.

MADAGASCAR

Home affairs are not talked
about on the public square.

NIGERIA

Old age does not
announce itself.

SOUTH AFRICA

A powerful leader adorns
his followers.

IVORY COAST AND TOGO

If you educate a man,
you educate an individual.
If you educate a woman,
you educate a nation.

GHANA

Learning expands great souls.

NAMIBIA

Have a small TV and
a big library!

4

Gifting Yourself
to Others

It was a cold morning as a mother drove her son to school. On the way, she saw one of his classmates walking to school and she stopped. Her son recognized the boy. It was John, a kid from the neighborhood.

"Why are you stopping? He can get to school by himself. After all, it is not all that cold," her son protested.

The mother ignored her son's advice and invited John to hop right in. In the car, her son completely ignored the boy. He was not from his circle of friends. When they got to school, her son jumped out and walked as far ahead of John as possible, so he didn't have to talk to him.

When he got home in the evening, there was a letter waiting for him at the table. He knew he was in trouble.

"What is it about you that makes you think you are more special than John? I want you to go and apologize to him first thing in school tomorrow."

Getting to the zone of exclusivity
requires little of us. But welcoming
strangers requires much more
and tests our core.

A candle burns itself out
to give light to others.

TOGO

If you want to go fast,
go alone.
If you want to go far,
go together.

GHANA

If there is cause to hate someone,
the cause to love has just begun.

SENEGAL AND GAMBIA

When you row another
person across the river,
you get there yourself.

TANZANIA

You cannot tell a hungry child
that you gave him food yesterday.

ZIMBABWE

He who talks incessantly
talks nonsense.

IVORY COAST

A butterfly that flies among
thorns will tear its wings.

LIBERIA AND EQUATORIAL GUINEA

Around a flowering tree,
there are many insects.

GUINEA

You should never forget your
neighbor when you invite
people to come to the feast.

KENYA

The axe forgets;
the tree remembers.

ZIMBABWE

Hope resides in togetherness.

SIERRA LEONE

You cannot create a community
when you are absent.

Friendship is honey—

but don't eat it all.

MOROCCO

If you take advantage of your
friends, you will be handing them
the scissors to cut you off.

Peace is costly but it is
worth the expense.

KENYA

If you destroy a bridge,
be sure you can swim.

ZANZIBAR

Rather than tell a lie to help a
friend, it is better to assist him in
paying the fine for his offense.

NIGERIA

Confiding a secret to an
unworthy person is like carrying
grain in a bag with a hole.

ETHIOPIA

To fight with everyone
can result in a shortage of
pallbearers at your funeral.

ETHIOPIA

A person is buried the way they lived.

When the fox dies, fowls
do not mourn.

KENYA

People are man's medicine.

SENEGAL

A camel does not make fun
of another camel's hump.

GHANA

Being grateful, a man
makes himself deserving of
yet another kindness.

NIGERIA

When the elephants fight,
it is the grass that suffers.

KENYA

The weak get hurt when
the powerful fight.

When a tiny toe is hurting,
the whole body stoops
down to attend to it.

NAMIBIA

Sweet tongues buy
horses on credit.

NIGERIA

You do not give a hyena
meat to watch over.

MAURITIUS

*Don't tempt a man through
his weaknesses.*

The earth is a beehive;
we all enter by the same door
but live in different cells.

CENTRAL AFRICAN REPUBLIC

When the bee comes to your
house, let her have beer;
you may want to visit the
bee's house someday.

DEMOCRATIC REPUBLIC
OF THE CONGO

A friend is someone you
share the path with.

UGANDA, SUDAN, AND CENTRAL
AFRICAN REPUBLIC

To have no enemies is
equivalent to wealth.

NIGERIA

If the cockroach wants to rule
over the chicken, then it must
hire a fox as a bodyguard.

SIERRA LEONE

*The enemy of your enemy
is your friend.*

A family is like a forest.
When you are outside, it is dense;
when you are inside, you see
that each tree has its place.

GHANA

Each family has its secrets.

In the moment of crisis,
the wise build bridges and
the foolish build dams.

NIGERIA

*To solve problems, think of ways
to bring people together instead
of creating divisions.*

In the birds' court,
a cockroach never wins his case.

RWANDA

*Do not expect justice when
your enemy is the judge.*

Do not tell the man who is
carrying you that he stinks.

SIERRA LEONE

A boat cannot go forward if
each rows his own way.

TANZANIA

A traveler to distant places
should make no enemies.

SWAZILAND

A person who sells eggs
should not start a fight
in the market.

KENYA

No matter how powerful a
man is, he cannot make the
rains fall on his farm alone.

CAMEROON

Nature is just.

Corn cannot get justice
in a chicken's court.

NIGERIA

If you escaped from
the lion's den, why go
back for your hat?

SOMALIA

A gentle word sends the sword
back into the scabbard.

NIGERIA

If you see a man in a gown
eating with a man in rags,
the food belongs to the latter.

MAURITANIA

If you play push with
the porcupine, expect
to get sore hands.

NIGER

Do a good deed and
throw it into the sea.

EGYPT

There is no medicine
to cure hatred.

GHANA

A bird will always use
another bird's feathers to
feather its own nest.

DEMOCRATIC REPUBLIC
OF THE CONGO

There is no better mirror
than a best friend.

CAPE VERDE

*Pick friends who will make
you a better person.*

Only the mountains never meet.

NAMIBIA

*Unlike mountains, people move
from place to place and you never
know who you will encounter.*

The nail never takes advice
from the hammer.

DEMOCRATIC REPUBLIC
OF THE CONGO

If you never offer palm wine
to your uncle, you will not
know many proverbs.

BENIN

A wound inflicted by a
friend does not heal.

DJIBOUTI

When the crocodile smiles,
be extra careful.

KENYA AND TANZANIA

Get your knowledge from
the minds of turtles.

TUNISIA

Learn from the elderly.
They have seen it all.

Between two friends, even
water drunk together is sweet.

GHANA

Suicide kills the people
who love you.

KENYA

While there is life, there is hope.

ETHIOPIA

An onion shared with a friend
tastes like roast lamb.

EGYPT

Equality is not easy,
but superiority is painful.

SENEGAL

All men were created equal.
It hurts to upset that equilibrium.

Sometimes the rain might force
a man more than once to seek
shelter under the same tree.

NIGERIA

Don't burn your bridges.

5

Your Sense of Passion

It is 6:30 on a cold Friday morning. I am having a quiet breakfast when suddenly the landline rings. I know where the call is coming from because no one in the United States calls me at that time and no one calls my landline anymore, except telemarketers—and my cousin. I answer the phone and I hear the distinctive voice of my cousin from Kenya. His voice comes across loud and clear, although he is more than eight thousand miles away.

There are two things I have explained to him repeatedly in the last ten years. First, he always calls me using my landline and, for some strange reason, he never uses my mobile phone no matter how many times I give the number to him. He is a businessman and owns two smartphones. I know both his numbers. But he somehow thinks my only phone is tethered to a wall! I guess that will only change after I do away with the landline someday. The second thing he does not seem to understand is the idea of time difference. It is not easy for someone in Africa to always remember that we are eight or nine hours behind in the Unites States, depending on the time of the year.

But this morning I will not mention either of those two things. There is no point. His call is a pleasant surprise and I am thrilled. He starts by asking me if I can recognize his voice. Of course, I can. His second question is more intriguing: Do I still remember that I am an alumnus of Nyaga Primary School, the elementary school that we both attended many years ago?

I visit the school whenever I go to Kenya and the question sets me on a nostalgic path down the memory lane to my childhood days. Nyaga Primary School was about two hundred yards from my grandmother's house where I grew up. Every morning, dressed in my khaki uniform, I would join a stream of other excited boys and girls walking to the school to get an education. As far as I can tell, of all the students who have passed through its gates since it opened in the early 1960s, I am the only one who went on to earn a PhD. Thinking about it now makes me feel enormously indebted to the institution. That's a matter of both pride and concern. It also unwittingly places a heavy burden and expectations on my shoulders.

"We want to buy books for the kids in the school. They do not have enough books," says my cousin. He explains that he has rounded up all the alumni he can find, and they have a month to raise the necessary funds.

"Count me in," I yell back.

He did not need to tell me what they were planning to do for the school. My answer will always be in the affirmative. How could I ever say "No" to such a request? I was once one of those boys: young, smart, happy, and surrounded by needs but seeing only hope ahead. I have walked in their shoes—except we had no shoes. I know what it is like to go barefoot to a urine-soaked bathroom and stand on the wet and soggy uncemented ground that reeks with the intoxicating stench of human urine. I would relieve myself, and still walk out with a wide smile totally oblivious to any health hazards, and grow up healthy, disease-free, strong, and vibrant.

Poverty gives you a deeper empathy.
You gain a sensitivity that allows you to have
compassion for others because you have
been where they are, you have walked in
their shoes, and if they have no shoes,
you know why, and you understand
what it is like to walk barefoot.

A happy man marries the girl
he loves, but a happier man
loves the girl he marries.

SENEGAL

The man may be the head
of the home but the wife is
the heart of the home.

KENYA

Outer beauty attracts the eyes,
but inner beauty
captivates the soul.

CAMEROON

Where love is, night
will never fall.

BURUNDI

It is better to fall and break
your back than to fall in love
and break your heart.

SEYCHELLES

Some wounds take too long to heal.

Pearls don't lie on the
seashore. If you want one,
you must dive for it.

ANGOLA, TANZANIA, AND KENYA

Love, like rain, does not choose
the grass on which it falls.

SOUTH AFRICA

The girl with stars in her eyes
will shine like the moonlight.

SOUTH AFRICA

*A happy person radiates
warmth to others.*

A beautiful thing is never perfect.

EGYPT

Love is a despot who

spares no one.

NAMIBIA

Happiness often sneaks in through
your door when left open.

KENYA

If a woman doesn't love you,
she calls you "brother."

IVORY COAST

Coffee and love taste
best when hot.

ETHIOPIA

Some things cannot wait.

To be able to love other people,
you must be able to love yourself.

DEMOCRATIC REPUBLIC
OF THE CONGO

*Take care of your needs first so you can
have the energy to give of yourself.*

A loved one has no pimples.

KENYA

The buttocks are like a married
couple; though there is constant
friction between them, they
still love and live together.

NIGERIA

A cheerful heart begets
increasing joy.

KENYA

People gravitate to happy people.

Love is like a baby:
it needs to be treated tenderly.

DEMOCRATIC REPUBLIC
OF THE CONGO

If the full moon loves you,
why worry about the stars?

TUNISIA

If you cannot hold children
in your arms, please hold
them in your heart.

UGANDA

*Love the vulnerable members of a
community. If you have nothing to give
them, just give them your love.*

A heart deep in love
has no patience.

TANZANIA

True love obeys no rules.

Having beauty does not mean
understanding the
perseverance of marriage.

NIGERIA

*Perseverance pays the bill
for the experience.*

Happiness is like a field you
can harvest every season.

A letter from the heart can
be read on the face.

When the heart acts, the
body is its slave.

EGYPT

It is much easier to fall in
love than to stay in love.

DEMOCRATIC REPUBLIC
OF THE CONGO

A man who hangs around a
beautiful girl without saying
a word ends up fetching water
for guests at her wedding.

NIGERIA

Marriage is like a groundnut;
you have to crack it to
see what is inside.

GHANA

The path to your heart's
desire is never overgrown.

UGANDA

You can win a woman
with lies but you cannot
feed her with lies.

COMOROS

Do not be so in love that
you cannot tell when
the rain is coming.

MADAGASCAR

Love is blind, but keep your senses.

Passion is of greater
consequence than facts.

ZIMBABWE

Passion has no reason.

Milk and honey have different
colors but they share the
same house peacefully.

TANZANIA

Love sees no color,
knows no color.

SOUTH AFRICA

Two noisy waterfalls do
not hear each other.

KENYA

Better to lose your eyes
than your heart.

TANZANIA

Kindness can pluck the hairs
of a lion's mustache.

SUDAN

Great men have big hearts.

ETHIOPIA

A good name is better
than good perfume.

ETHIOPIA

It is better to be loved
than feared.

SIERRA LEONE

A house cannot be repaired when
the owner is destroying it.

KENYA

A home is made of a shared vision.

Happiness is not perfected
until it is shared.

SOUTH AFRICA

A single bracelet does not jingle.

DEMOCRATIC REPUBLIC
OF THE CONGO

A woman is attractive when
she is somebody else's wife.

ZIMBABWE

What you give you get,
ten times over.

NIGERIA

Every rope has two ends.

GAMBIA

The most beautiful fig

may contain a worm.

SOUTH AFRICA

Appearances can be deceiving.

Greatness and beauty do not
belong to the gods alone.

NIGERIA

A wise fish should know that
a beautiful earthworm that looks
so easy to swallow has a sharp
hook attached to it.

SENEGAL

Patience puts a crown
on the head.

UGANDA

You can take the lid off a pot
to see what is inside, but
a person has no lid.

CAPE VERDE

If love is a sickness,
patience is the remedy.

CAMEROON

If you truly love somebody,
with time they will appreciate it.

There is always a better man
for every good man.

SOMALIA

Be content with what you have.

The quarrel of lovers is
the renewal of love.

MOROCCO

We should talk while
we are still alive.

KENYA

Dialogue protects life.

KENYA

Reason through differences.

6

A Love of
Knowing

After John Thuo's mother died, he ran away from home to escape the beatings from his cruel father. He'd make a playground of the streets of Nairobi, Kenya, which were often the scenes of horrendous traffic jams that usually brought the city to a crawl. In the congested streets, he was at the mercy of the vagaries of nature and suspicious citizens who often regarded street kids as thieves. On this particular day, the young street boy was moving from car to car begging for money.

He approached Gladys Kamande, seated in a nearby car, when he saw something he had never seen before. The woman was hooked up to tubes and was breathing from a portable tank. She explained to John that her lungs were not working well and she had to carry oxygen at all times. John was shocked. He could not believe that there was someone in the world who was worse off than he was. He started to cry and offered the lady the few pennies he had collected that day.

What John did not know was that Gladys was the victim of awful domestic violence that resulted in not only her breathing problems but also partial blindness and several miscarriages. In fact, she was on her way to a hospital appointment the day they met. Her family was also struggling to raise $54,000, which was needed for specialized treatment abroad.

Completely touched by what Gladys was going through, John reached out and held her hand through the open window. A passerby captured the tender moment on camera and uploaded the pictures online along with their story. Within days the incident went viral and thousands of online donations poured in. Eighty thousand dollars was raised, enabling Gladys to travel to India for medical treatment. And Nissy Wambugu, a complete stranger, opened her home to John, enrolled him in school, and became his adoptive mother. The kindness and compassion that John had extended to Gladys came back to him a hundredfold.

*What we give to the world is
what we receive in return.*

A flea can trouble a lion more
than a lion can trouble a flea.

KENYA

Sorrow is like rice in an attic—
you use a little every day and
soon it will be all gone.

MADAGASCAR

A leopard is chasing us, and
you are asking me,
"Is it a male or a female?"

BOTSWANA

The man who has bread to
eat does not appreciate the
severity of a famine.

NIGERIA

The tears running down your
face do not blind you.

ERITREA

*Your moment of sadness
will not last forever.*

Into a closed mouth,

no fly will enter.

MOROCCO

I never learned anything
while I was talking.

When one is in trouble,
one remembers God.

NIGERIA

When God cooks,
you don't see smoke.

ZAMBIA

You cannot convince a
monkey that honey is
sweeter than a banana.

GUINEA

No matter how beautiful
and well-crafted a coffin
might look, it will not make
anyone wish for death.

MOZAMBIQUE

When your luck deserts you,
even cold food burns.

Fire and gunpowder do
not sleep together.

No one drinks medicine on
behalf of a sick person.

SOUTH AFRICA

*Sometimes we have to let the people
we love carry their own burden.*

A fortune-teller says,
"If it is not a boy, it is a girl."

MADAGASCAR

If you're peeling groundnuts
for a blind man, you must keep
whistling so that he's sure
you are not eating them.

SOUTH AFRICA

When it is time for a
monkey to die, every tree
becomes very slippery.

KENYA

*You cannot run away
from your fate.*

A lie has many variations;
the truth, none.

DJIBOUTI

The one chased away with a club
comes back, but the one chased
away with reason does not.

KENYA

In a community of beggars,
stealing and not begging,
is considered a crime.

GHANA

What is inflated too much
will burst into fragments.

GABON

If you want to improve your
memory, lend someone money.

ZAMBIA

If you are looking for a fly
in your food, it means
that you are full.

SOUTH AFRICA

God himself chases the flies
away from tailless animals.

BENIN

Wisdom is not like money
to be tied up and hidden.

GHANA

Even the best dancer on the
stage must retire sometime.

NIGERIA

Every reign must come to an end.

You cannot shave a man's
head in his absence.

NIGER

*A matter cannot be settled
if the people concerned
are not present.*

If you refuse to stop fighting,
you cannot refuse to
show the wounds.

BURUNDI

There is many a good tune
played on an old fiddle.

NAMIBIA

The mouse that makes jest of a cat
has already seen a hole nearby.

NIGERIA

No one tests the depth of
a river with both feet.

GHANA

The bee is the doctor of flowers.

DEMOCRATIC REPUBLIC
OF THE CONGO

Remember, after the storm,
there will be a rainbow.

SUDAN, UGANDA, AND ETHIOPIA

An orphaned calf licks
its own back.

KENYA

*It is a tough life when
you are all alone.*

It is the calm and silent
water that drowns a man.

KENYA

*Sometimes situations that you expect
to be safe can spring a surprise on you
and turn out to be dangerous.*

It is better to walk than
curse the road.

*Deal with the problem instead
of complaining.*

It is the one who lies by a fire
who can feel how hot it is.

BOTSWANA

When the lion is crippled,
the hare goes to his house
for debt recovery.

MOZAMBIQUE

Even without drumbeats,
tree leaves dance.

DEMOCRATIC REPUBLIC
OF THE CONGO

We are slaves to our routines.

An egg never sits on a hen.

UGANDA AND KENYA

The universe has its natural order.

Do not rush the night.
The sun will always rise
for its own sake.

You cannot push the river.
It will flow on its own.

The zebra told the white horse,
"I am white," and told the black
horse, "I am actually black."

NAMIBIA

*Don't conform to other people's
expectations; stay true to yourself.*

Death is like an eagle that
snatches away a chick and
leaves its mother in tears.

COMOROS

There is no god like
one's stomach; we must
succumb to it every day.

BENIN

You cannot take away
someone's luck.

KENYA

A ripened fruit does not
cling to the vine.

ZIMBABWE

He who is unable to dance
says that the yard is stony.

KENYA

Excuses conceal weaknesses.

The squirrel does not talk
back to the elephant.

ANGOLA

Where there is shame,
there is no honor.

ETHIOPIA

When you have a lot to do,
start with a meal.

SOUTH AFRICA

Always taking out and
never putting in soon
reaches the bottom.

SWAZILAND

Wisdom is like fire.
People borrow it from others.

DEMOCRATIC REPUBLIC
OF THE CONGO

*In traditional African societies, fire was
produced from a special wood or stone and
community members could take it freely from
anyone who had it. Similarly, the elders and
the wise share their knowledge and pass it
on freely through stories and proverbs.*

No matter how old the cow is,
his liver is not old.

SIERRA LEONE

*Do not underestimate the value
of an elderly person.*

Every knot has an
unraveler in God.

EGYPT

A wise man who knows proverbs
reconciles difficulties.

GHANA

Dogs do not actually prefer
bones to meat. It is just that no
one ever gives them meat.

GHANA

Maize yields better for
those without teeth.

ZAMBIA

A strawberry doesn't
ripen according to the
wishes of a baboon.

LESOTHO

*Things don't always happen
according to one's wishes.*

Proverbs are the palm oil with
which words are eaten.

NIGERIA

The world does not make
promises to anybody.

DJIBOUTI

Even drumsticks are
heavy on the way home
after the dance.

NIGER

Burdens are heavier at the end
of the journey.

Despite the beauty of the moon,
sun, and the stars, the sky
also has a threatening thunder
and striking lightning.

NIGERIA

Life serves every dose in two forms—
happiness and sadness;
life and death.

The pillar of the world is hope.

TANZANIA

Life is God's best gift;
the rest is what you make of it.

TANZANIA

Last Thought

There was an old man in the village who was a long-distance trader. He bought farm produce from surrounding villages and sold it in the capital city. He would spend the entire day trading food in the city, but he never bought himself a meal. Instead, he would wait to go home in the evening and eat. He invested his money in land, shares, and stocks. When he died, the doctors said the cause of death was malnutrition!

His kids inherited his wealth and squandered it all in less than five years.

*It is rewarding to work hard, but be
sure to take time out to enjoy your life
and the fruits of your labor. Life is
about finding the right balance.*

Acknowledgments

I am profoundly grateful to the ancestors for their wisdom. May this light from the other world illuminate our paths.

I would like to extend my deep gratitude to my literary agent, Lawrence Jordan, for his mentorship and guidance throughout this project as I worked to extract the gems from the ore.

I am profoundly grateful to my wife, Nancy Wairimu, and to my children, Erwin Chege and Ethan Chege, for their support and encouragement and for serving as my sounding boards.

My sincere gratitude to my editor, Tracy Sherrod, for her long and sustained interest in this book. Her vision and feedback were invaluable in shaping this final product.

About the Author

Sam Chege was born and raised in Kenya. In his thirties he immigrated to the United States, where he has lived for more than twenty years. He is an associate professor of journalism and mass communications at Kansas State University.